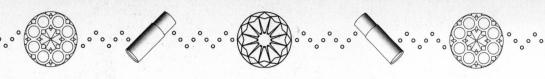

Kaleidoscope
Math

by Cindi Mitchell and Jim Mitchell

S C H O L A S T I C
PROFESSIONAL BOOKS

New York ○ **Toronto** ○ **London** ○ **Auckland** ○ **Sydney**

New Delhi ○ **Mexico City** ○ **Hong Kong** ○ **Buenos Aires**

To Connie Stoll, Steve Mitchell, and Dave Mitchell,
the best of luck and love always.

Special thanks to our son, Ben Mitchell, for his assistance with rendering the art for this book.

Cover design by Norma Ortiz
Interior design and illustrations by Jim Mitchell,
except pages 6–8 by James Graham Hale

ISBN: 0-439-08675-2
Copyright © 2003 by Cindi Mitchell and Jim Mitchell
Published by Scholastic Inc.
All rights reserved.
Printed in U.S.A.

4 5 6 7 8 9 10   40   09 08 07 06

Contents

Multiplication and Division

Continued

Decimals and Fractions

About This Book

Say the word *kaleidoscope* and images of dazzling, colorful repeating patterns come to mind. Kaleidoscopes have fascinated children and adults alike since they were first invented in the early 1800s.

Sir David Brewster was a scientist who studied the principles of light. He was fascinated by what happened when light was reflected. Brewster carefully placed three mirrors in a tube and attached a rotating chamber to hold pieces of broken colored glass. The results were marvelous. The images viewed when gazing into the tube were vibrant, ever-changing geometric collages formed by the reflections of the broken glass in the mirrors.

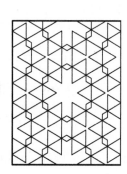

Brewster applied for a patent and marketed his creation as a toy. The inventor put three Greek words together to name the toy: *kalos*, beautiful; *eidos*, form; and *skopeo*, I see. Most people would agree that the images and colors reflected by this simple device are, indeed, beautiful forms to see!

In this book you will find a collection of kaleidoscopic images for your students to color and enjoy. Each activity consists of two pages, a kaleidoscope picture page and a worksheet of math problems. First, students solve the math problems on the worksheet. Then they look at the corresponding page, find the answers to the problems, and color the shapes as indicated on the worksheet. All your students will need to complete these activities are colored pencils or crayons and a regular pencil.

You may wish to use the activities in this book to reinforce basic math skills. To further extend the math, science, and art connection, you may want to introduce some of the basic principles of reflection and have students make a simple kaleidoscope before beginning the activity pages. You'll find directions for a more in-depth look at this topic on the following pages.

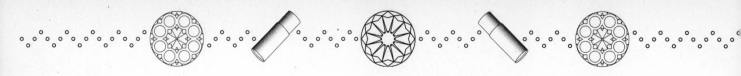

Kaleidoscope Basics

Through the use of mirrors, kaleidoscopes create multiple repeating images and patterns. To figure out how kaleidoscopes work, it is best to start with a hinged mirror and a protractor. (See Resources, page 9.) If you do not have hinged mirrors, students can create their own:

1. Place two mirrors side by side, facedown on a flat surface. Tape the backs of the mirrors together, leaving a tiny space between them. This will create a hinge.

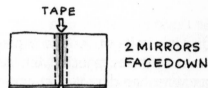

2. To begin, have students place an object between the hinged mirrors. Then position the mirrors at various angles and help children determine how many reflections they see. They should notice that the number of images increases as the angle of the mirrors decreases.

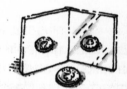

3. Then invite students to make a 45° angle on a sheet of paper, using their protractors. Place the hinged part of the mirror on the vertex of the angle and line up the edges of the mirrors on the sides of the angle. Place an object between the mirrors. Ask students to count the number of images they see. (*eight*) Point out that they can find the number of objects mathematically by dividing 360 degrees by the number of degrees in the angle. For instance, in the example above, the angle is 45°. 360° ÷ 45° = 8

4. Have students draw 60°, 90°, and 120° angles. Place the hinged mirrors on top of each angle and have them count the number of images. (*60°, six; 90°, four; 120°, three*)

5. As students begin using the activity pages, encourage them to use their set of mirrors to explore the designs before coloring them. For example, in Diamond Patch (page 20), have them measure one of the angles using a protractor. (*60°*) How many triangles will be formed when the mirrors are at a 60° angle? (*360° ÷ 60° = 6; there are six triangles.*)

6. Ask students how many images they see in the mirrors. (*six*) Have them remove the mirrors and look at the whole page. They will notice that the image in the mirrors and the image on the paper are identical—both show six triangles inside. Students can repeat this exploration with Hexagon Puzzle (page 60).

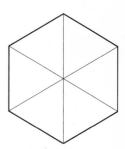

7. Now invite students to experiment with Navajo Star (page 10) and Wagon Wheel (page 58). Ask them to predict how many images they will see when they line up the mirrors with the sides of one triangular image on each of these designs. Then have students test to find out. (*Navajo Star: 12, Wagon Wheel: 12*)

8. Have students look at these kaleidoscopic images: Colorful Spotlights (page 42) and Twirling Windmills (page 54). Guide them to notice that these patterns do not form a circular or hexagonal shape. These reflections are classified as wallpaper patterns; the designs extend forever in both the vertical and horizontal direction.

9. Finally, have students form a 60° angle with the edges of the hinged mirrors and place an object between the mirrors. Have them place a third mirror on the open end of the mirrors and notice what happens to the images. (An infinite pattern appears.) Point out that most kaleidoscopes are made with three mirrors placed at 60° angles.

How to Make a Kaleidoscope

Once students have experimented with the hinged mirrors, invite them to make their own kaleidoscopes.

1. Place the three mirrors facedown on a flat surface. Leave a small space between them so that they form a triangle after they are taped.

2. Cut two lengths of tape as long as the edge of the mirrors. First, press one piece of tape firmly on the edge of two of the mirrors so that it holds them together. Then tape the third mirror to the second.

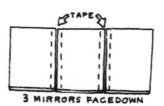

TAPE

3 MIRRORS FACEDOWN

Materials
• 3 small, identical square or rectangular mirrors (*see Resources, page 9*)
• tape
• glue
• white bond paper
• scraps of colored paper, sequins, glitter, or beads
• plastic wrap
• scissors
<u>Optional</u>: wrapping paper, construction paper, or wallpaper samples

3. Stand the mirrors up, keeping the taped sides out. Fold the mirrors inward to form a triangle. Cut another piece of tape and tape the last two edges together. Trim excess tape from the top and bottom.

4. Put a small amount of glue on the top edges of the mirrors. Set the glued edges on a piece of white paper. After the glue has dried, trim the remaining paper from the sides of the kaleidoscope.

5. Place scraps of paper, sequins, glitter, or beads inside the kaleidoscope.

6. Cut a piece of plastic wrap a little bigger than the triangle opening. Pull it tight over the opening and hold it in place with a rubber band. Tape the edges of the plastic wrap in place.

7. Students can decorate the outside of the kaleidoscope with wrapping paper, construction paper, or wallpaper samples, if desired.

8. Now it's time to have fun with the kaleidoscopes! Have students shake them up and watch the shapes tumble around inside, making beautiful reflections. Encourage students to hold their kaleidoscopes up to the light of the window or take them outside. Ask students to look in the kaleidoscope and find the six-sided hexagon shape and the mirrored reflections. Remind them of their explorations with Diamond Patch, Hexagon Puzzle, Navajo Star, and Wagon Wheel. What similarities do they notice between those designs and the kaleidoscopic images?

Resources

Supply Sources

The following companies sell kaleidoscopes and small mirrors that can be used to make kaleidoscopes. You can also find inexpensive square or rectangular mirrors at craft and art supply stores, as well as hardware, educational supply, and discount stores.

Delta Education
hinged mirrors, rectangular mirrors, and kaleidoscopes
800-258-1302
www.delta-education.com

School Mart
hinged mirrors
800-285-2662
www.schoolmart.com

Franklin Art Glass
kaleidoscope kits, rectangular and square mirrors
800-848-7683

ETA—A Universe of Learning
hinged mirrors, tessellation kaleidoscope kits
800-445-5985
www.etacuisenaire.com

S & S Crafts
kaleidoscope kits
800-243-9232
www.snswwide.com

Books

Kaleidoscopes: Wonders of Wonder by Cozy Baker (C & T Publishing, 1999).
Filled with colorful kaleidoscopic images, this book explores the art and science behind kaleidoscopes.

The Kids' Book of Kaleidoscopes by Carolyn Bennet and Jack Romig (Workman Publishing Co., 1994).
This full-color activity book and kit explains the principles of light refraction and reflection and includes everything you need to make a kaleidoscope.

The Kaleidoscope Book: A Spectrum of Spectacular Scopes to Make by Thom Boswell (Lark Books, 1995).
Readers learn how kaleidoscopes work and how to make their own simple kaleidoscopes.

Software

KaleidoMania! developed by Kevin D. Lee (Key Curriculum Press).
With this exciting software tool, you can make your own symmetrical designs or ones based on pictures included on the CD-ROM. Also includes games that investigate rotation, reflection, and more.

Name _____

Navajo Star

Solve the problems. Then, on page 11, find the shape(s) with each answer, and color them as directed below. (Hint: Look carefully—some of the answers are written in more than one shape!) Finally, fill in any remaining shapes with colors of your choice.

Color the shapes dark red.

12 × 5	41 × 7	88 × 6	25 × 9	17 × 8
24 × 3	32 × 2	70 × 4	67 × 2	44 × 2
53 × 3	10 × 9			

Color the shapes blue.

82 × 2	80 × 6	38 × 2	41 × 9	81 × 8
29 × 3	12 × 8	93 × 7	11 × 3	28 × 7
77 × 4	40 × 9			

Name _____

Navajo Star

Name_____

Blooming Flower

Solve the problems. Then, on page 13, find the shape(s) with each answer, and color them as directed below. (Hint: Look carefully—some of the answers are written in more than one shape!) Finally, fill in any remaining shapes with colors of your choice.

Color the shapes blue.

312 × 5	141 × 7	187 × 4	129 × 9
712 × 8	293 × 7	611 × 3	128 × 7

Color the shapes light blue.

364 × 3	437 × 2	370 × 4	269 × 2
820 × 6	838 × 4	541 × 9	811 × 8

Color the shapes green.

244 × 3	312 × 2	710 × 4	637 × 2
144 × 6	174 × 2	117 × 8	249 × 7

Color the shapes yellow.

382
× 2

Color the shapes pink.

429
× 3

Name _____

Blooming Flower

Name _____

Exotic Circles

Solve the problems. Then, on page 15, find the shape(s) with each answer, and color them as directed below. (Hint: Look carefully—some of the answers are written in more than one shape!) Finally, fill in any remaining shapes with colors of your choice.

Color the shapes dark red.

$$\begin{array}{r} 31 \\ \times\ 15 \\ \hline \end{array} \qquad \begin{array}{r} 11 \\ \times\ 27 \\ \hline \end{array} \qquad \begin{array}{r} 18 \\ \times\ 34 \\ \hline \end{array} \qquad \begin{array}{r} 73 \\ \times\ 10 \\ \hline \end{array} \qquad \begin{array}{r} 12 \\ \times\ 41 \\ \hline \end{array}$$

Color the shapes blue.

$$\begin{array}{r} 34 \\ \times\ 13 \\ \hline \end{array} \qquad \begin{array}{r} 43 \\ \times\ 82 \\ \hline \end{array} \qquad \begin{array}{r} 33 \\ \times\ 31 \\ \hline \end{array} \qquad \begin{array}{r} 37 \\ \times\ 42 \\ \hline \end{array} \qquad \begin{array}{r} 26 \\ \times\ 52 \\ \hline \end{array}$$

Color the shapes yellow.

$$\begin{array}{r} 24 \\ \times\ 13 \\ \hline \end{array} \qquad \begin{array}{r} 31 \\ \times\ 22 \\ \hline \end{array} \qquad \begin{array}{r} 41 \\ \times\ 39 \\ \hline \end{array} \qquad \begin{array}{r} 18 \\ \times\ 94 \\ \hline \end{array} \qquad \begin{array}{r} 37 \\ \times\ 52 \\ \hline \end{array}$$

Color the shapes purple.

$$\begin{array}{r} 82 \\ \times\ 12 \\ \hline \end{array} \qquad \begin{array}{r} 71 \\ \times\ 28 \\ \hline \end{array} \qquad \begin{array}{r} 82 \\ \times\ 36 \\ \hline \end{array} \qquad \begin{array}{r} 29 \\ \times\ 47 \\ \hline \end{array} \qquad \begin{array}{r} 24 \\ \times\ 57 \\ \hline \end{array} \qquad \begin{array}{r} 12 \\ \times\ 17 \\ \hline \end{array}$$

Color the shapes orange.

$$\begin{array}{r} 41 \\ \times\ 23 \\ \hline \end{array} \qquad \begin{array}{r} 61 \\ \times\ 38 \\ \hline \end{array} \qquad \begin{array}{r} 14 \\ \times\ 46 \\ \hline \end{array} \qquad \begin{array}{r} 17 \\ \times\ 52 \\ \hline \end{array} \qquad \begin{array}{r} 17 \\ \times\ 62 \\ \hline \end{array}$$

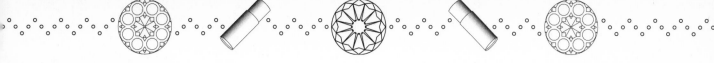

Name _____

Exotic Circles

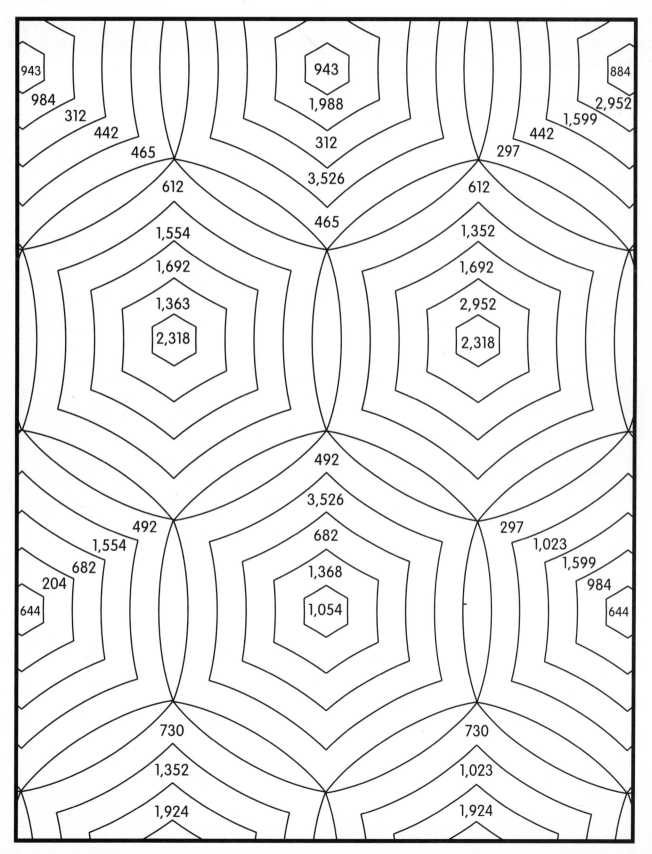

Name _____

Morning Star

Solve the problems. Then, on page 17, find the shape(s) with each answer, and color them as directed below. (Hint: Look carefully—some of the answers are written in more than one shape!) Finally, fill in any remaining shapes with colors of your choice.

Color the shapes orange.

531	912	128	723	313
× 10	× 11	× 12	× 15	× 18

227	435	503	319	624
× 24	× 44	× 33	× 25	× 52

Color the shapes dark red.

444	651	870	231	126
× 23	× 32	× 31	× 13	× 22

Color the shapes red.

912	821	712	623	125
× 19	× 23	× 37	× 27	× 47

Color the shapes yellow.

740	712	128	422	307
× 43	× 39	× 46	× 52	× 42

Name _____

Morning Star

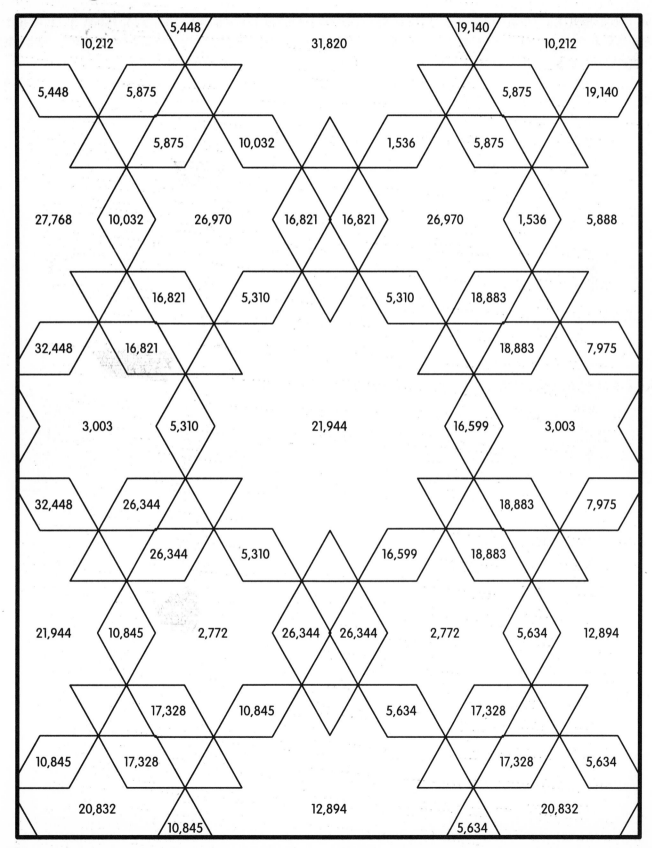

Name _____

Nigerian Plate

Solve the problems. Then, on page 19, find the shape(s) with each answer, and color them as directed below. (Hint: Look carefully—some of the answers are written in more than one shape!) Finally, fill in any remaining shapes with colors of your choice.

Color the shapes orange.

$2\overline{)188}$ $7\overline{)245}$ $8\overline{)152}$ $5\overline{)130}$

Color the shapes purple.

$3\overline{)135}$ $8\overline{)168}$ $9\overline{)135}$ $3\overline{)117}$

Color the shapes yellow.

$2\overline{)176}$ $4\overline{)244}$ $6\overline{)312}$ $9\overline{)387}$

Color the shapes blue.

$8\overline{)576}$ $6\overline{)150}$ $4\overline{)132}$ $7\overline{)280}$

Color the shapes dark red.

$3\overline{)234}$ $5\overline{)480}$ $2\overline{)164}$ $8\overline{)248}$

Color the shapes green.

$6\overline{)282}$ $2\overline{)198}$ $7\overline{)476}$ $9\overline{)333}$

Color the shapes pink.

$3\overline{)207}$ $4\overline{)300}$ $8\overline{)400}$ $7\overline{)294}$

Name _____

Nigerian Plate

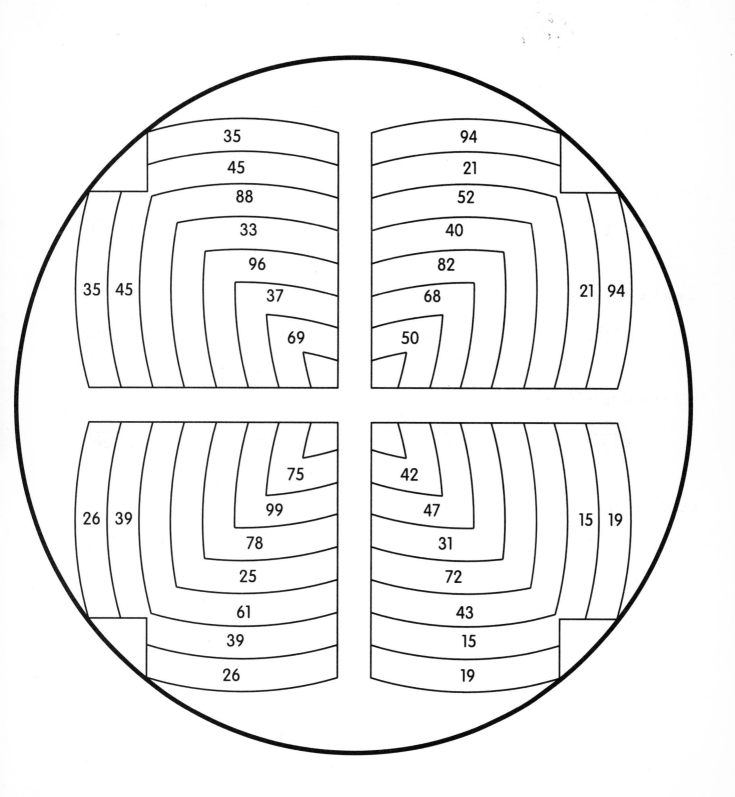

Name _____

Diamond Patch

Solve the problems. Then, on page 21, find the shape(s) with each answer, and color them as directed below. (Hint: Look carefully—some of the answers are written in more than one shape!) Finally, fill in any remaining shapes with colors of your choice.

Color the shapes dark red.

$2\overline{)189}$ $\qquad$ $3\overline{)125}$ $\qquad$ $5\overline{)149}$ $\qquad$ $4\overline{)149}$

$6\overline{)242}$ $\qquad$ $8\overline{)318}$ $\qquad$ $9\overline{)140}$ $\qquad$ $7\overline{)202}$

Color the shapes yellow.

$3\overline{)190}$ $\qquad$ $7\overline{)191}$ $\qquad$ $8\overline{)236}$ $\qquad$ $4\overline{)193}$

$9\overline{)206}$ $\qquad$ $3\overline{)172}$ $\qquad$ $5\overline{)154}$ $\qquad$ $6\overline{)401}$

Color the shapes light green.

$2\overline{)183}$ $\qquad$ $9\overline{)196}$ $\qquad$ $7\overline{)258}$ $\qquad$ $8\overline{)149}$

$6\overline{)303}$ $\qquad$ $3\overline{)170}$

Color the shapes light orange.

$2\overline{)159}$

Name _____

Diamond Patch

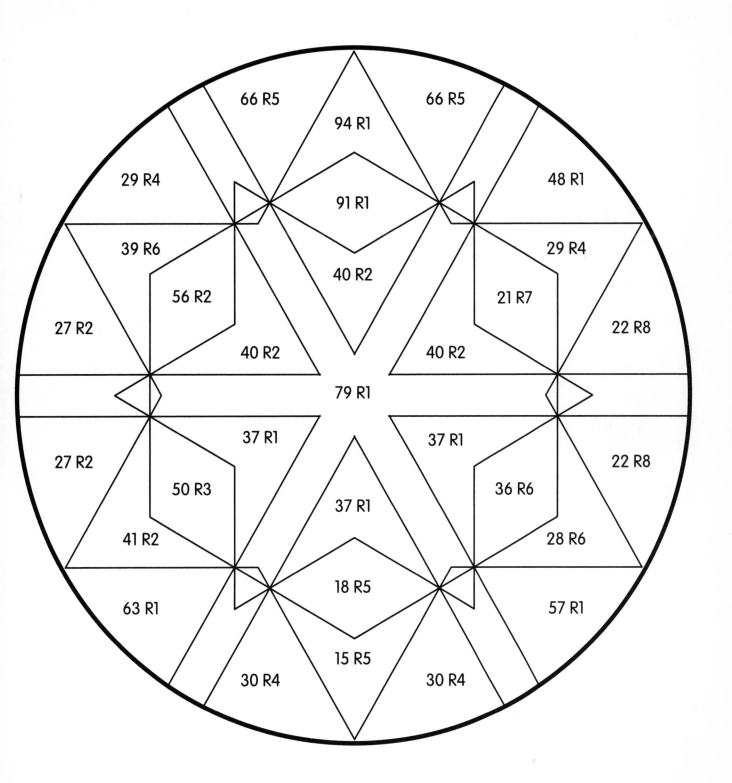

66 R5 66 R5

94 R1

29 R4 48 R1

91 R1

39 R6 29 R4

40 R2

56 R2 21 R7

27 R2 22 R8

40 R2 40 R2

79 R1

27 R2 22 R8

37 R1 37 R1

50 R3 36 R6

37 R1

41 R2 28 R6

18 R5

63 R1 57 R1

15 R5

30 R4 30 R4

Name _____

Eight-Pointed Star

Solve the problems. Then, on page 23, find the shape(s) with each answer, and color them as directed below. (Hint: Look carefully—some of the answers are written in more than one shape!) Finally, fill in any remaining shapes with colors of your choice.

Color the shapes pink.

$$8 \overline{)86} \qquad 9 \overline{)276} \qquad 5 \overline{)254} \qquad 4 \overline{)283}$$

Color the shapes dark red.

$$7 \overline{)282} \qquad 4 \overline{)322} \qquad 9 \overline{)548} \qquad 6 \overline{)125}$$

Color the shapes orange.

$$6 \overline{)303} \qquad 9 \overline{)92} \qquad 8 \overline{)161} \qquad 2 \overline{)141}$$

Color the shapes purple.

$$3 \overline{)607} \qquad 5 \overline{)549} \qquad 2 \overline{)521} \qquad 7 \overline{)761}$$

Color the shapes green.

$$2 \overline{)209}$$

Color the shapes light blue.

$$5 \overline{)511}$$

Name _____

Eight-Pointed Star

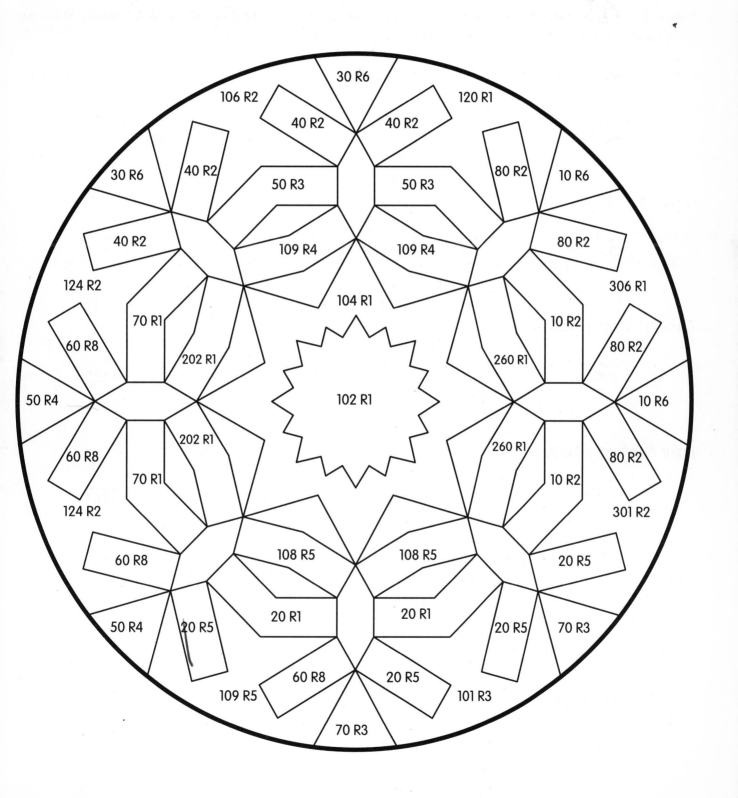

Name _____

Triangle Patches

Solve the problems. Then, on page 25, find the shape(s) with each answer, and color them as directed below. (Hint: Look carefully—some of the answers are written in more than one shape!) Finally, fill in any remaining shapes with colors of your choice.

Color the shapes green.

$62\overline{)310}$ $\qquad$ $41\overline{)246}$ $\qquad$ $15\overline{)135}$

$23\overline{)161}$ $\qquad$ $37\overline{)111}$ $\qquad$ $56\overline{)224}$

Color the shapes yellow.

$97\overline{)194}$ $\qquad$ $74\overline{)592}$ $\qquad$ $29\overline{)348}$

$35\overline{)525}$ $\qquad$ $27\overline{)567}$ $\qquad$ $45\overline{)585}$

Color the shapes orange.

$36\overline{)828}$ $\qquad$ $29\overline{)551}$ $\qquad$ $18\overline{)450}$

$26\overline{)910}$ $\qquad$ $19\overline{)323}$ $\qquad$ $28\overline{)868}$

Color the shapes dark red.

$21\overline{)882}$ $\qquad$ $25\overline{)825}$ $\qquad$ $22\overline{)616}$

$12\overline{)612}$ $\qquad$ $11\overline{)704}$ $\qquad$ $42\overline{)924}$

Name _____

Triangle Patches

25

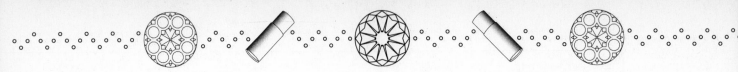

Name_____

Queen's Crown

Solve the problems. Then, on page 27, find the shape(s) with each answer, and color them as directed below. (Hint: Look carefully—some of the answers are written in more than one shape!) Finally, fill in any remaining shapes with colors of your choice.

Color the shapes green.

$$46 \overline{)232} \qquad 46 \overline{)279} \qquad 15 \overline{)149} \qquad 29 \overline{)156}$$

Color the shapes blue.

$$88 \overline{)357} \qquad 37 \overline{)133} \qquad 41 \overline{)300} \qquad 99 \overline{)232}$$

Color the shapes yellow.

$$91 \overline{)195} \qquad 31 \overline{)270} \qquad 32 \overline{)311} \qquad 29 \overline{)189}$$

Color the shapes light orange.

$$39 \overline{)526} \qquad 37 \overline{)813} \qquad 24 \overline{)575} \qquad 31 \overline{)582}$$

Color the shapes red.

$$12 \overline{)911} \qquad 15 \overline{)922} \qquad 22 \overline{)614} \qquad 27 \overline{)842}$$

Queen's Crown

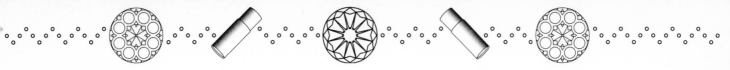

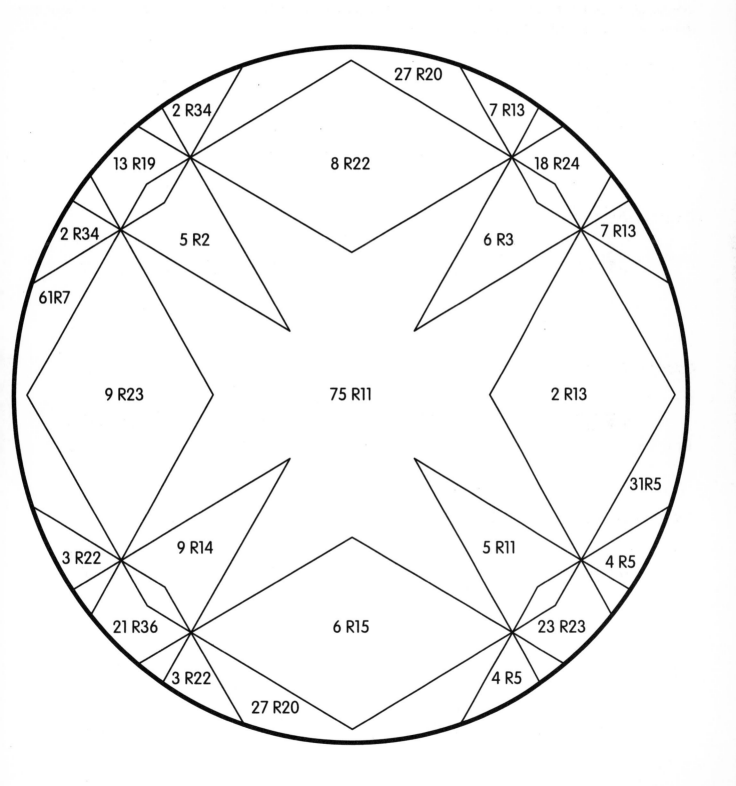

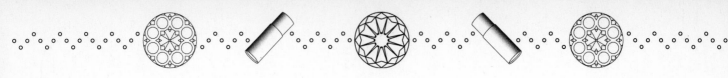

Name _____

Rose Wallpaper

Find the average. Then, on page 29, find the shape(s) with each answer, and color them as directed below. (Hint: Look carefully—some of the answers are written in more than one shape!) Finally, fill in any remaining shapes with colors of your choice.

Color the shapes pink.

13, 12, 14 _____   25, 19, 22 _____   3, 12, 19, 6 _____

54, 66 _____   22, 18, 56 _____   6, 12, 20, 10 _____

Color the shapes blue.

16, 14 _____   112, 100 _____   7, 10, 12, 15 _____

23, 45, 16 _____   30, 60 _____   9, 15, 30 _____

Color the shapes yellow.

100, 108 _____   25, 25, 22 _____   40, 20, 10, 30 _____

99, 27 _____   88, 86, 84 _____   10, 26, 15, 13 _____

Color the shapes light blue.

10, 50 _____   108, 20, 58 _____   7, 8, 8, 9 _____

40, 45, 43, 40 _____

Name _____

Rose Wallpaper

Name _____

Twinkling Star

Circle the larger number in each pair of decimals. Then, on page 31, find the shape(s) with each circled decimal, and color them as directed below. (Hint: Look carefully—some of the answers are written in more than one shape!) Finally, fill in any remaining shapes with colors of your choice.

Color the shapes light orange.

| 8.4   8.9 | 34.7   34.2 | 62.74   62.09 | 0.13   1.3 |

| 5.6   5.42 | 72.13   72.3 | 102.65   102.6 | 56.5   5.65 |

Color the shapes yellow.

| 8.30   8.03 | 3.75   3.7 | 9.1   0.91 | 7.7   7.07 |

| 0.04   0.4 | 99.3   99.18 | 2.05   2.50 | 3.5   3.44 |

Color the shapes dark red.

| 7.8   7.79 | 1.7   0.17 | 5.01   5.10 | 4.07   4.70 |

| 0.09   0.9 | 8.1   8.11 | 1.05   1.5 | 9.7   9.47 |

Color the shapes blue.

| 119.76   119.67 |

Name _____

Decimals: Comparing

Twinkling Star

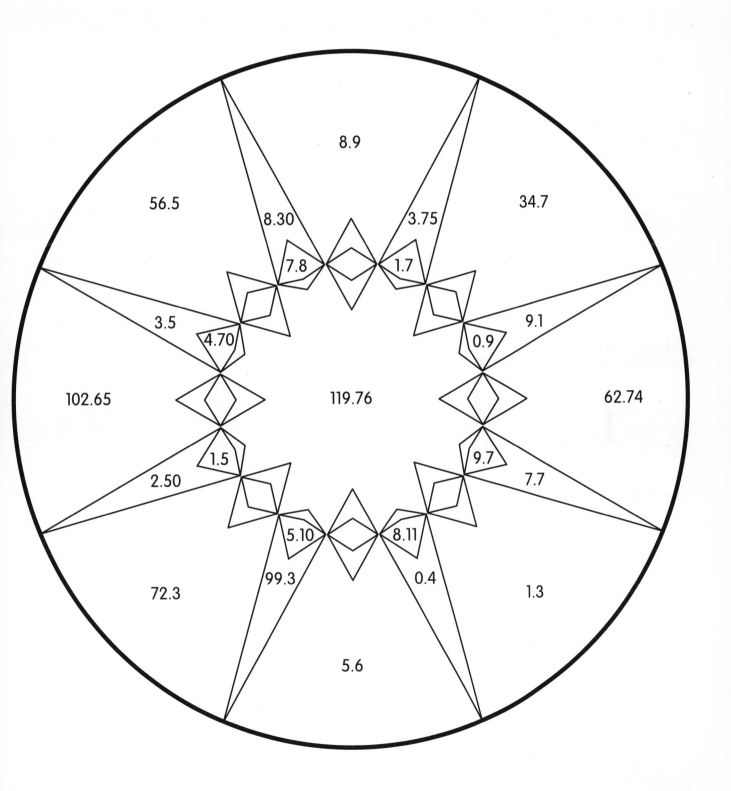

8.9

56.5

8.30

3.75

34.7

7.8

1.7

3.5

4.70

9.1

0.9

102.65

119.76

62.74

1.5

9.7

2.50

7.7

5.10

8.11

99.3

0.4

72.3

1.3

5.6

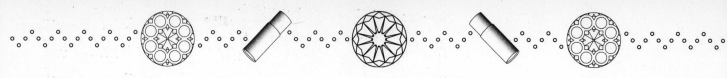

Name_____

Blazing Arrows

Round each decimal as directed below. Then, on page 33, find the shape(s) with each answer, and color them as directed below. (Hint: Look carefully—some of the answers are written in more than one shape!)

Round each decimal to the nearest whole number. Color the shapes dark red.

4.8 _____   8.3 _____   18.1 _____   32.5 _____

Round each decimal to the nearest whole number. Color the shapes yellow.

24.6 _____   11.3 _____   9.9 _____   0.6 _____

Round each decimal to the nearest tenth. Color the shapes pink.

34.87 _____   0.51 _____   29.32 _____   0.77 _____

Round each decimal to the nearest tenth. Color the shapes purple.

80.86 _____   0.344 _____   7.84 _____   45.062 _____

Round each decimal to the nearest hundredth. Color the shapes light blue.

44.089 _____   5.301 _____   8.948 _____   0.255 _____

Round each decimal to the nearest hundredth. Color the shapes blue.

2.373 _____   4.221 _____   0.933 _____   1.439 _____

Round the dollar amount to the nearest dollar. Color the shape green.

$99.72 _____

Round the dollar amount to the nearest dollar. Color the shape light green.

$94.22 _____

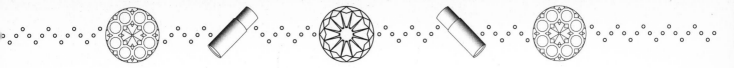

Name _____

Blazing Arrows

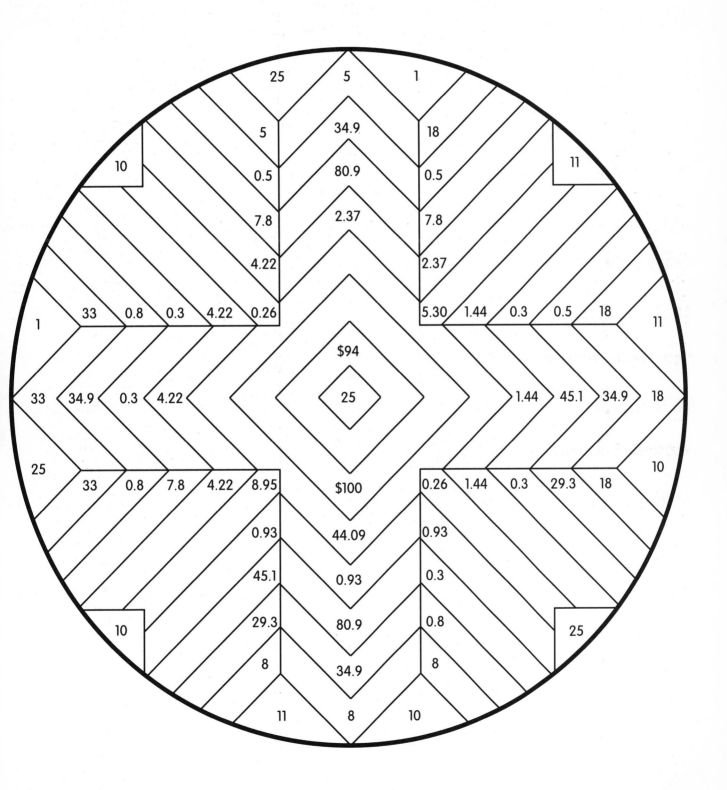

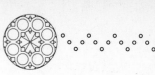

Name _____

Twirling Pinwheels

Solve the problems. Then, on page 35, find the shape(s) with each answer, and color them as directed below. (Hint: Look carefully—some of the answers are written in more than one shape!)

Color the shapes dark red.

82.3	7.16	6.38	23.7
+ 17.0	+ 1.13	+ 6.61	+ 73.7

Color the shapes orange.

3.67	3.53	65.3	72.3
+ 8.21	+ 4.19	+ 15.2	+ 32.4

Color the shapes red.

69.5	3.55	48.2	1.12
+ 5.3	+ 6.19	+ 18.7	+ 7.38

Color the shapes blue.

9.305	34.53	2.48	6.993
+ 2.352	+ 75.34	+ 1.37	+ 5.002

Color the shapes green.

65.19	46.1	70.37	5.26
+ 13.46	+ 53.5	+ 29.02	+ 4.57

Color the shapes yellow.

57.9	8.74	72.06	2.803
+ 37.0	+ 0.18	+ 24.05	+ 5.119

Name _____

Twirling Pinwheels

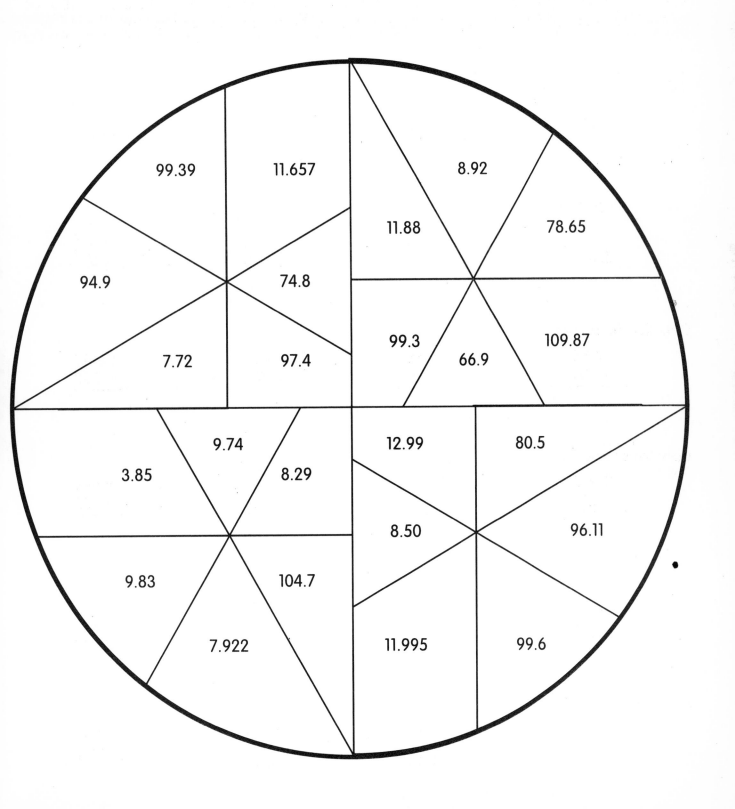

99.39 11.657 8.92

11.88 78.65

94.9 74.8

99.3 109.87

7.72 97.4 66.9

9.74 12.99 80.5

3.85 8.29

8.50 96.11

9.83 104.7

7.922 11.995 99.6

Name _____

Stars and Squares

Solve the problems. Then, on page 37, find the shape(s) with each answer, and color them as directed below. (Hint: Look carefully—some of the answers are written in more than one shape!) Finally, fill in any remaining shapes with colors of your choice.

Color the shapes dark red.

69.3 − 13.0	9.18 − 7.13	6.98 − 6.61	99.8 − 63.7
8.50 − 3.21	4.53 − 2.19	75.0 − 24.9	85.3 − 52.4
63.5 − 15.1	7.55 − 6.27	67.9 − 8.7	8.42 − 7.38

Color the shapes blue.

9.305 − 8.152	73.59 − 65.35	2.44 − 1.37	3.293 − 2.892
65.99 − 17.66	76.9 − 68.5	70.37 − 29.02	8.96 − 4.57
47.9 − 39.0	6.74 − 0.18	62.28 − 24.25	7.809 − 5.139

Name _____

Stars and Squares

Name_____

Stained-Glass Window

Solve the problems. Then, on page 39, find the shape(s) with each answer, and color them as directed below. (Hint: Look carefully—some of the answers are written in more than one shape!)

Color the shapes blue.

6.0	7.2	12	8.3	52
× 1.1	× 4.5	× 1.7	× 4.9	× 8.9

Color the shapes dark red.

402	7.8	332	14.2	9.7
× 0.3	× 12	× 1.7	× 8.9	× 2.3

Color the shapes red.

1.28	15.7	31.2	74.2	9.9
× 0.4	× 3.3	× 0.06	× 0.6	× 6.9

Color the shapes green.

4.7	11.7	0.4	1.8	13.7
× 6.9	× 0.9	× 2.8	× 4.3	× 2.9

Color the shapes yellow.

3.7	1.3	2.2	1.4	2.0
× 0.6	× 1.2	× 3.1	× 7.1	× 4.2

Color the shapes orange.

28.1	1.12	33.2	201.2	21.02
× 1.3	× 0.9	× 0.2	× 2.3	× 0.4

Stained-Glass Window

120.6   0.512

6.64

0.512   120.6

32.4

6.6

120.6

120.6

8.4

8.4

120.6

0.512

7.74

0.512

0.512

7.74

0.512

8.4

8.4

8.4

120.6

2.22

120.6

0.512   120.6

39.73

120.6   0.512

1.008

1.008

32.4   120.6

1.56

120.6   6.6

8.4

8.4

0.512

1.12

51.81

51.81

1.12

0.512

564.4

8.4

8.4

93.6

564.4   51.81

36.53

51.81   93.6

564.4   40.67

20.4   93.6

8.4

8.4

68.31

10.53

51.81

51.81

10.53

1.872

8.4

8.4

126.38   6.82

22.31

68.31   126.38

39.73

22.31   1.872

462.76

40.67   126.38   9.94

22.31   20.4

8.408

8.4

8.4

68.31

32.43

44.52

44.52

32.43

1.872

8.4

8.4

126.38   462.8

462.8   22.31

36.53

126.38   44.52

44.52   22.31

Name _____

Firecracker

Write the equivalent fraction. Then, on page 41, find the shape(s) with each answer, and color them as directed below. (Hint: Look carefully—some of the answers are written in more than one shape!) Finally, fill in any remaining shapes with colors of your choice.

Color the shapes green.

$$\frac{1}{2} = \frac{8}{}$$ $$\frac{2}{3} = \frac{10}{}$$ $$\frac{3}{5} = \frac{}{10}$$ $$\frac{1}{5} = \frac{5}{}$$ $$\frac{1}{4} = \frac{}{20}$$

$$\frac{3}{4} = \frac{9}{}$$ $$\frac{7}{9} = \frac{}{27}$$ $$\frac{7}{8} = \frac{}{16}$$ $$\frac{1}{11} = \frac{5}{}$$ $$\frac{6}{7} = \frac{}{49}$$

Color the shapes light green.

$$\frac{1}{9} = \frac{9}{}$$ $$\frac{4}{5} = \frac{16}{}$$ $$\frac{4}{7} = \frac{}{63}$$ $$\frac{1}{8} = \frac{4}{}$$ $$\frac{2}{9} = \frac{}{45}$$

$$\frac{6}{7} = \frac{42}{}$$ $$\frac{4}{9} = \frac{32}{}$$ $$\frac{3}{5} = \frac{}{15}$$ $$\frac{8}{9} = \frac{16}{}$$ $$\frac{1}{2} = \frac{}{8}$$

Color the shapes yellow-green.

$$\frac{1}{3} = \frac{9}{}$$ $$\frac{2}{9} = \frac{10}{}$$ $$\frac{3}{4} = \frac{}{32}$$ $$\frac{1}{11} = \frac{4}{}$$ $$\frac{1}{9} = \frac{}{72}$$

$$\frac{5}{12} = \frac{20}{}$$ $$\frac{2}{10} = \frac{10}{}$$ $$\frac{10}{11} = \frac{}{33}$$ $$\frac{6}{7} = \frac{30}{}$$ $$\frac{1}{4} = \frac{}{28}$$

Color the shapes yellow.

$$\frac{1}{13} = \frac{2}{}$$ $$\frac{3}{4} = \frac{30}{}$$ $$\frac{1}{5} = \frac{}{10}$$ $$\frac{8}{9} = \frac{48}{}$$ $$\frac{1}{2} = \frac{}{26}$$

Color the shapes light orange.   Color the shapes orange.   Color the shapes dark orange.

$$\frac{5}{6} = \frac{50}{}$$ $$\frac{5}{8} = \frac{25}{}$$ $$\frac{1}{5} = \frac{5}{}$$

Name _____

Firecracker

Name _____

Colorful Spotlights

Rename each fraction in lowest terms. Then, on page 43, find the shape(s) with each answer, and color them as directed below. (Hint: Look carefully—some of the answers are written in more than one shape!) Finally, fill in any remaining shapes with colors of your choice.

Color the shapes orange.

$\frac{2}{4}$ = _____ $\frac{5}{20}$ = _____ $\frac{9}{12}$ = _____ $\frac{10}{15}$ = _____

$\frac{14}{16}$ = _____ $\frac{18}{20}$ = _____ $\frac{6}{15}$ = _____ $\frac{2}{14}$ = _____

Color the shapes red.

$\frac{9}{81}$ = _____ $\frac{9}{15}$ = _____ $\frac{4}{32}$ = _____ $\frac{12}{21}$ = _____

$\frac{14}{49}$ = _____ $\frac{9}{24}$ = _____ $\frac{16}{18}$ = _____ $\frac{20}{25}$ = _____

Color the shapes green.

$\frac{9}{27}$ = _____ $\frac{24}{56}$ = _____ $\frac{10}{24}$ = _____ $\frac{6}{30}$ = _____

$\frac{3}{39}$ = _____ $\frac{35}{56}$ = _____ $\frac{30}{35}$ = _____ $\frac{18}{81}$ = _____

Color the shapes blue.

$\frac{12}{40}$ = _____ $\frac{15}{18}$ = _____ $\frac{16}{36}$ = _____ $\frac{5}{35}$ = _____

$\frac{42}{54}$ = _____ $\frac{2}{12}$ = _____ $\frac{15}{27}$ = _____ $\frac{5}{50}$ = _____

Name _____

Colorful Spotlights

$\frac{3}{10}$	$\frac{1}{3}$	$\frac{3}{10}$		$\frac{3}{10}$	$\frac{1}{3}$	$\frac{5}{6}$		$\frac{5}{6}$	$\frac{3}{7}$	$\frac{5}{6}$
		$\frac{1}{9}$	$\frac{3}{10}$	$\frac{1}{9}$		$\frac{3}{5}$	$\frac{5}{6}$	$\frac{3}{5}$		
	$\frac{1}{2}$		$\frac{3}{7}$		$\frac{1}{4}$		$\frac{5}{12}$		$\frac{3}{4}$	
		$\frac{1}{8}$	$\frac{4}{9}$	$\frac{1}{8}$		$\frac{4}{7}$	$\frac{1}{7}$	$\frac{4}{7}$		
$\frac{4}{9}$	$\frac{5}{12}$	$\frac{4}{9}$		$\frac{4}{9}$	$\frac{1}{5}$	$\frac{1}{7}$		$\frac{1}{7}$	$\frac{1}{5}$	$\frac{1}{7}$
		$\frac{1}{8}$	$\frac{4}{9}$	$\frac{1}{8}$		$\frac{4}{7}$	$\frac{1}{7}$	$\frac{4}{7}$		
	$\frac{2}{3}$		$\frac{1}{13}$		$\frac{7}{8}$		$\frac{1}{13}$		$\frac{9}{10}$	
		$\frac{2}{7}$	$\frac{1}{6}$	$\frac{2}{7}$		$\frac{3}{8}$	$\frac{5}{9}$	$\frac{3}{8}$		
$\frac{1}{6}$	$\frac{5}{8}$	$\frac{1}{6}$		$\frac{1}{6}$	$\frac{5}{8}$	$\frac{5}{9}$		$\frac{5}{9}$	$\frac{6}{7}$	$\frac{5}{9}$
		$\frac{2}{7}$	$\frac{1}{6}$	$\frac{2}{7}$		$\frac{3}{8}$	$\frac{5}{9}$	$\frac{3}{8}$		
	$\frac{2}{5}$		$\frac{6}{7}$		$\frac{1}{7}$		$\frac{6}{7}$		$\frac{1}{7}$	
		$\frac{8}{9}$	$\frac{1}{10}$	$\frac{8}{9}$		$\frac{4}{5}$	$\frac{7}{9}$	$\frac{4}{5}$		
$\frac{1}{10}$	$\frac{2}{9}$	$\frac{1}{10}$		$\frac{1}{10}$	$\frac{2}{9}$	$\frac{7}{9}$		$\frac{7}{9}$	$\frac{2}{9}$	$\frac{7}{9}$

Name _____

Mosaic Star

Rewrite each improper fraction as a mixed number. Then, on page 45, find the shape(s) with each answer, and color them as directed below. (Hint: Look carefully—some of the answers are written in more than one shape!) Finally, fill in any remaining shapes with colors of your choice.

Color the shapes red.

$\frac{7}{2}$ = _____ $\frac{13}{3}$ = _____ $\frac{9}{4}$ = _____

$\frac{17}{3}$ = _____ $\frac{45}{6}$ = _____ $\frac{18}{5}$ = _____

Color the shapes light orange.

$\frac{19}{9}$ = _____ $\frac{51}{8}$ = _____ $\frac{12}{5}$ = _____

$\frac{83}{9}$ = _____ $\frac{21}{10}$ = _____ $\frac{32}{7}$ = _____

Color the shapes blue.

$\frac{53}{8}$ = _____ $\frac{64}{7}$ = _____ $\frac{19}{15}$ = _____

$\frac{17}{12}$ = _____ $\frac{25}{8}$ = _____ $\frac{56}{11}$ = _____

Color the shapes light green.

$\frac{20}{7}$ = _____ $\frac{50}{11}$ = _____ $\frac{56}{5}$ = _____

$\frac{89}{9}$ = _____ $\frac{21}{5}$ = _____ $\frac{11}{3}$ = _____

Color the shapes yellow.

$\frac{25}{23}$ = _____

Name_____

Mosaic Star

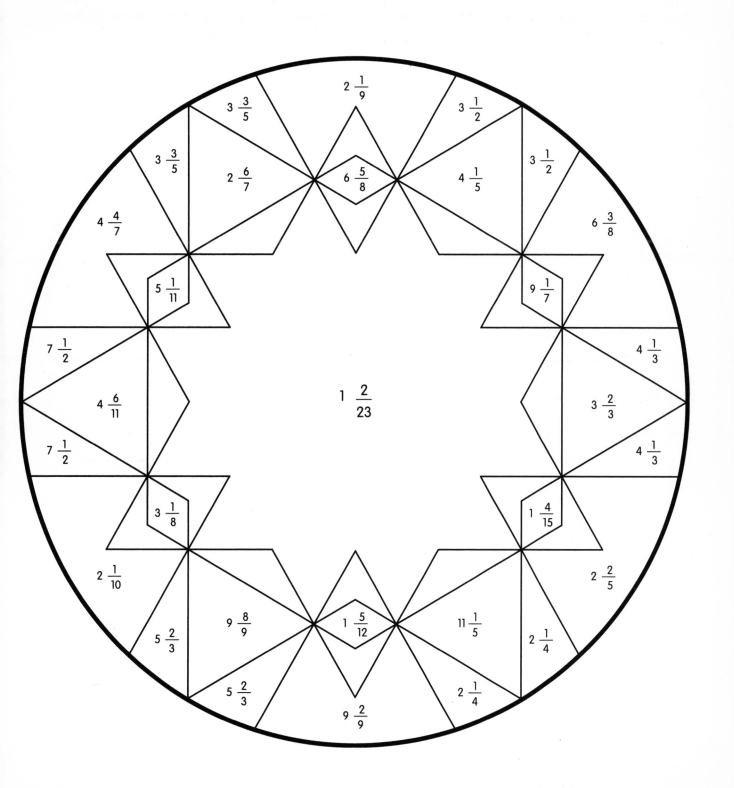

Name _____

Starry Hexagons

Rewrite each whole number or mixed number as an improper fraction. Then, on page 47, find the shape(s) with each answer, and color them as directed below. (Hint: Look carefully—some of the answers are written in more than one shape!) Finally, fill in any remaining shapes with colors of your choice.

Color the shapes orange.

$8\frac{1}{2}$ = _____ $5 = \dfrac{}{3}$ $2 = \dfrac{}{9}$ $4 = \dfrac{}{8}$

$2\frac{1}{6}$ = _____ $8\frac{3}{4}$ = _____ $4\frac{2}{5}$ = _____ $7 = \dfrac{}{3}$

Color the shapes red.

$2\frac{5}{7}$ = _____ $9\frac{1}{9}$ = _____ $7\frac{1}{2}$ = _____ $6\frac{5}{7}$ = _____

$14 = \dfrac{}{1}$ $9\frac{1}{3}$ = _____ $6\frac{5}{6}$ = _____ $9 = \dfrac{}{5}$

Color the shapes light blue.

$1\frac{1}{9}$ = _____ $5\frac{2}{3}$ = _____ $4\frac{1}{5}$ = _____ $4\frac{1}{2}$ = _____

$4\frac{3}{4}$ = _____ $6 = \dfrac{}{7}$ $15 = \dfrac{}{1}$ $3\frac{3}{8}$ = _____

Color the shapes green.

$9\frac{1}{2}$ = _____ $3\frac{1}{9}$ = _____ $1\frac{7}{10}$ = _____ $8\frac{2}{3}$ = _____

Color the shapes purple.

$3 = \dfrac{}{2}$ $13 = \dfrac{}{1}$ $10 = \dfrac{}{6}$ $1 = \dfrac{}{5}$

Name _____

Starry Hexagons

$\frac{60}{6}$ $\frac{60}{6}$ $\frac{15}{2}$ $\frac{13}{1}$ $\frac{13}{1}$ $\frac{82}{9}$ $\frac{60}{6}$ $\frac{60}{6}$

$\frac{21}{3}$ $\frac{21}{3}$ $\frac{18}{9}$ $\frac{18}{9}$

$\frac{19}{7}$ $\frac{19}{7}$ $\frac{15}{1}$ $\frac{15}{3}$ $\frac{13}{1}$ $\frac{17}{3}$ $\frac{13}{1}$ $\frac{15}{3}$ $\frac{21}{5}$ $\frac{15}{2}$ $\frac{15}{2}$

$\frac{18}{9}$ $\frac{18}{9}$ $\frac{19}{7}$ $\frac{19}{2}$ $\frac{47}{7}$ $\frac{13}{6}$ $\frac{13}{6}$

$\frac{13}{1}$ $\frac{13}{1}$ $\frac{13}{1}$ $\frac{13}{1}$ $\frac{6}{2}$ $\frac{6}{2}$

$\frac{19}{7}$ $\frac{15}{3}$ $\frac{15}{3}$ $\frac{47}{7}$

$\frac{10}{9}$ $\frac{13}{1}$ $\frac{18}{9}$ $\frac{42}{7}$ $\frac{45}{5}$ $\frac{45}{5}$ $\frac{19}{4}$ $\frac{13}{6}$ $\frac{6}{2}$ $\frac{9}{2}$

$\frac{41}{6}$ $\frac{32}{8}$ $\frac{32}{8}$ $\frac{15}{2}$

$\frac{13}{1}$ $\frac{28}{9}$ $\frac{13}{1}$ $\frac{5}{5}$ $\frac{5}{5}$ $\frac{15}{2}$ $\frac{28}{9}$ $\frac{6}{2}$

$\frac{18}{9}$ $\frac{18}{9}$ $\frac{41}{6}$ $\frac{13}{6}$ $\frac{13}{6}$

$\frac{28}{3}$ $\frac{28}{3}$ $\frac{10}{9}$ $\frac{32}{8}$ $\frac{5}{5}$ $\frac{9}{2}$ $\frac{5}{5}$ $\frac{32}{8}$ $\frac{21}{5}$ $\frac{82}{9}$ $\frac{82}{9}$

$\frac{35}{4}$ $\frac{35}{4}$ $\frac{14}{1}$ $\frac{28}{9}$ $\frac{19}{7}$ $\frac{35}{4}$ $\frac{35}{4}$

$\frac{13}{1}$ $\frac{13}{1}$ $\frac{5}{5}$ $\frac{5}{5}$ $\frac{6}{2}$ $\frac{6}{2}$

$\frac{14}{1}$ $\frac{32}{8}$ $\frac{32}{8}$ $\frac{19}{7}$

$\frac{27}{8}$ $\frac{13}{1}$ $\frac{35}{4}$ $\frac{17}{3}$ $\frac{47}{7}$ $\frac{47}{7}$ $\frac{9}{2}$ $\frac{35}{4}$ $\frac{6}{2}$ $\frac{21}{5}$

$\frac{19}{7}$ $\frac{17}{2}$ $\frac{17}{2}$ $\frac{14}{1}$

$\frac{17}{10}$ $\frac{13}{1}$ $\frac{6}{2}$ $\frac{26}{3}$ $\frac{6}{2}$

$\frac{13}{1}$ $\frac{13}{1}$ $\frac{5}{5}$ $\frac{5}{5}$

$\frac{35}{4}$ $\frac{35}{4}$ $\frac{19}{7}$ $\frac{14}{1}$ $\frac{35}{4}$ $\frac{35}{4}$

$\frac{82}{9}$ $\frac{82}{9}$ $\frac{15}{1}$ $\frac{17}{2}$ $\frac{5}{5}$ $\frac{42}{7}$ $\frac{5}{5}$ $\frac{17}{2}$ $\frac{10}{9}$ $\frac{15}{2}$ $\frac{15}{2}$

$\frac{22}{5}$ $\frac{22}{5}$ $\frac{15}{2}$ $\frac{47}{7}$ $\frac{22}{5}$ $\frac{22}{5}$

$\frac{60}{6}$ $\frac{60}{6}$ $\frac{5}{5}$ $\frac{17}{10}$ $\frac{5}{5}$ $\frac{60}{6}$ $\frac{60}{6}$

Name _____

Circle of Bows

Solve the problems and rename the fractions in lowest terms. Then, on page 49, find the shape(s) with each answer, and color them as directed below. (Hint: Look carefully—some of the answers are written in more than one shape!) Finally, fill in any remaining shapes with colors of your choice.

Color the shapes red.

$$\frac{2}{5} + \frac{2}{5} = \underline{\hspace{2cm}}$$ $$\frac{4}{11} + \frac{4}{11} = \underline{\hspace{2cm}}$$ $$\frac{5}{10} + \frac{4}{10} = \underline{\hspace{2cm}}$$

Color the shapes orange.

$$\frac{3}{8} + \frac{2}{8} = \underline{\hspace{2cm}}$$ $$\frac{3}{12} + \frac{2}{12} = \underline{\hspace{2cm}}$$ $$\frac{1}{10} + \frac{6}{10} = \underline{\hspace{2cm}}$$

Color the shapes blue.

$$\frac{2}{9} + \frac{5}{9} = \underline{\hspace{2cm}}$$ $$\frac{3}{12} + \frac{3}{12} = \underline{\hspace{2cm}}$$ $$\frac{1}{3} + \frac{1}{3} = \underline{\hspace{2cm}}$$

Color the shapes green.

$$\frac{1}{8} + \frac{1}{8} = \underline{\hspace{2cm}}$$ $$\frac{2}{7} + \frac{4}{7} = \underline{\hspace{2cm}}$$ $$\frac{1}{6} + \frac{4}{6} = \underline{\hspace{2cm}}$$

Color the shapes yellow.

$$\frac{2}{12} + \frac{5}{12} = \underline{\hspace{2cm}}$$ $$\frac{1}{16} + \frac{1}{16} = \underline{\hspace{2cm}}$$ $$\frac{4}{18} + \frac{4}{18} = \underline{\hspace{2cm}}$$

Color the shapes purple.

$$\frac{3}{12} + \frac{6}{12} = \underline{\hspace{2cm}}$$ $$\frac{1}{11} + \frac{1}{11} = \underline{\hspace{2cm}}$$ $$\frac{1}{7} + \frac{4}{7} = \underline{\hspace{2cm}}$$

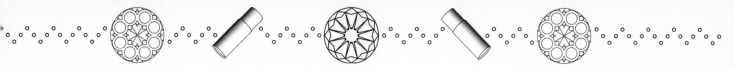

Name _____

Circle of Bows

Name_____

Rows of Daisies

Solve the problems and rename the fractions in lowest terms. Then, on page 51, find the shape(s) with each answer, and color them as directed below. (Hint: Look carefully—some of the answers are written in more than one shape!) Finally, fill in any remaining shapes with colors of your choice.

Color the shapes light orange.

$\frac{1}{3} + \frac{1}{2} = $ _____

$\frac{5}{12} + \frac{1}{4} = $ _____

$\frac{1}{6} + \frac{2}{9} = $ _____

$\frac{3}{8} + \frac{1}{2} = $ _____

$\frac{1}{2} + \frac{1}{12} = $ _____

$\frac{1}{2} + \frac{4}{10} = $ _____

Color the shapes blue.

$\frac{5}{10} + \frac{1}{5} = $ _____

$\frac{1}{7} + \frac{1}{3} = $ _____

$\frac{1}{3} + \frac{1}{6} = $ _____

$\frac{1}{8} + \frac{1}{4} = $ _____

$\frac{2}{12} + \frac{1}{4} = $ _____

$\frac{2}{10} + \frac{3}{5} = $ _____

Color the shapes dark red.

$\frac{1}{4} + \frac{3}{8} = $ _____

$\frac{4}{9} + \frac{1}{3} = $ _____

$\frac{5}{12} + \frac{2}{6} = $ _____

$\frac{2}{7} + \frac{1}{3} = $ _____

$\frac{1}{3} + \frac{2}{9} = $ _____

$\frac{2}{5} + \frac{1}{3} = $ _____

Name _____

Rows of Daisies

$\frac{5}{8}$ 7/8 $\frac{5}{8}$	$\frac{5}{12}$	$\frac{5}{12}$	$\frac{13}{21}$ 7/8 $\frac{5}{9}$

$\frac{5}{12}$ $\frac{5}{8}$ $\frac{5}{12}$ $\frac{13}{21}$ $\frac{5}{6}$ $\frac{13}{21}$ $\frac{5}{12}$ $\frac{11}{15}$ $\frac{5}{12}$

$\frac{13}{21}$ $\frac{13}{21}$

$\frac{7}{9}$ $\frac{2}{3}$ $\frac{3}{8}$ $\frac{13}{21}$ $\frac{4}{5}$ $\frac{7}{18}$ $\frac{5}{9}$

$\frac{7}{9}$ $\frac{3}{4}$ $\frac{11}{15}$ $\frac{5}{9}$

$\frac{3}{8}$ $\frac{7}{9}$ $\frac{3}{8}$ $\frac{7}{8}$ $\frac{4}{5}$ $\frac{11}{15}$ $\frac{4}{5}$

$\frac{3}{4}$ $\frac{3}{4}$

$\frac{7}{9}$ $\frac{7}{12}$ $\frac{1}{2}$ $\frac{3}{4}$ $\frac{7}{10}$ $\frac{9}{10}$ $\frac{7}{9}$

$\frac{7}{9}$ $\frac{7}{9}$ $\frac{3}{4}$ $\frac{7}{9}$

$\frac{1}{2}$ $\frac{7}{9}$ $\frac{1}{2}$ $\frac{7}{8}$ $\frac{7}{10}$ $\frac{7}{9}$ $\frac{7}{10}$

$\frac{3}{4}$ $\frac{3}{4}$

$\frac{3}{4}$

$\frac{3}{4}$ 7/8 $\frac{10}{21}$ $\frac{10}{21}$ 7/8 $\frac{7}{9}$

Name _____

Flower Petal

Solve the problems and rename the fractions in lowest terms. Then, on page 53, find the shape(s) with each answer, and color them as directed below. (Hint: Look carefully—some of the answers are written in more than one shape!) Finally, fill in any remaining shapes with colors of your choice.

Color the shapes dark orange.

$$\frac{6}{9} - \frac{1}{9} = \underline{\hspace{2cm}} \qquad \frac{5}{5} - \frac{1}{5} = \underline{\hspace{2cm}} \qquad \frac{5}{12} - \frac{4}{12} = \underline{\hspace{2cm}}$$

Color the shapes light orange.

$$\frac{3}{9} - \frac{2}{9} = \underline{\hspace{2cm}} \qquad \frac{5}{6} - \frac{4}{6} = \underline{\hspace{2cm}} \qquad \frac{8}{11} - \frac{2}{11} = \underline{\hspace{2cm}}$$

Color the shapes light yellow.

$$\frac{12}{14} - \frac{7}{14} = \underline{\hspace{2cm}} \qquad \frac{10}{12} - \frac{2}{12} = \underline{\hspace{2cm}} \qquad \frac{9}{10} - \frac{6}{10} = \underline{\hspace{2cm}}$$

Color the shapes light blue.

$$\frac{8}{8} - \frac{4}{8} = \underline{\hspace{2cm}} \qquad \frac{6}{7} - \frac{4}{7} = \underline{\hspace{2cm}} \qquad \frac{8}{9} - \frac{6}{9} = \underline{\hspace{2cm}}$$

Color the shapes purple.

$$\frac{9}{10} - \frac{2}{10} = \underline{\hspace{2cm}} \qquad \frac{12}{16} - \frac{2}{16} = \underline{\hspace{2cm}} \qquad \frac{3}{15} - \frac{1}{15} = \underline{\hspace{2cm}}$$

Name _____

Flower Petal

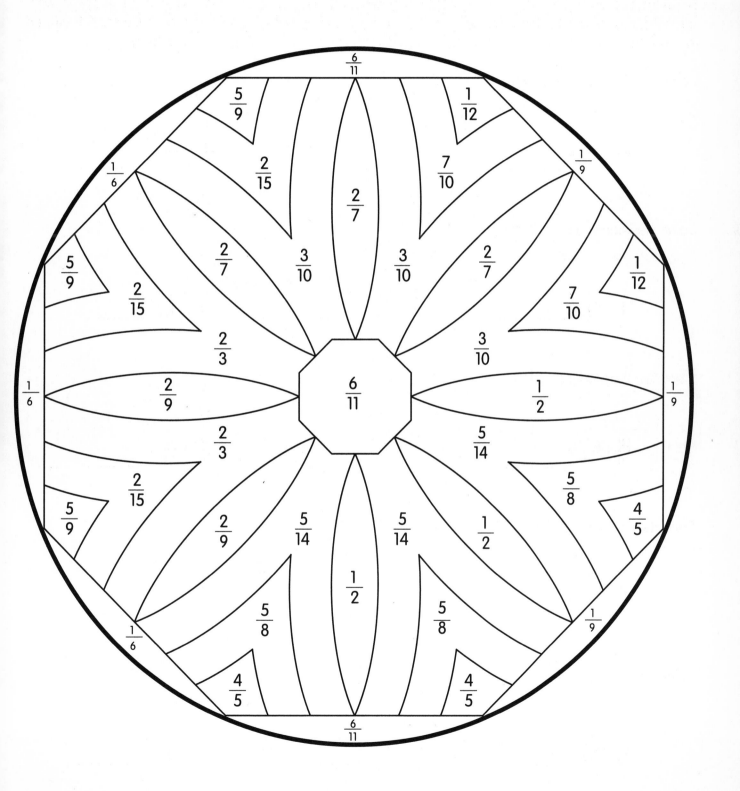

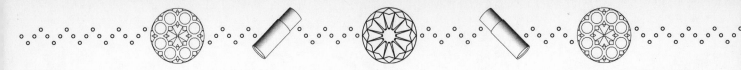

Fractions: Subtraction With
Unlike Denominators

Twirling Windmills

Solve the problems and rename the fractions in lowest terms. Then, on page 55, find the shape(s) with each answer, and color them as directed below. (Hint: Look carefully—some of the answers are written in more than one shape!) Finally, fill in any remaining shapes with colors of your choice.

Color the shapes light orange.

$\frac{7}{10} - \frac{1}{2} =$ _____ $\frac{4}{5} - \frac{1}{10} =$ _____ $\frac{5}{6} - \frac{1}{3} =$ _____

$\frac{5}{8} - \frac{2}{4} =$ _____ $\frac{9}{10} - \frac{1}{2} =$ _____ $\frac{1}{2} - \frac{2}{8} =$ _____

Color the shapes yellow.

$\frac{12}{14} - \frac{1}{2} =$ _____ $\frac{4}{6} - \frac{1}{2} =$ _____ $\frac{7}{9} - \frac{1}{3} =$ _____

$\frac{5}{6} - \frac{3}{12} =$ _____ $\frac{3}{10} - \frac{1}{5} =$ _____ $\frac{9}{10} - \frac{3}{5} =$ _____

Color the shapes blue.

$\frac{2}{3} - \frac{1}{9} =$ _____ $\frac{7}{8} - \frac{1}{4} =$ _____ $\frac{5}{8} - \frac{1}{4} =$ _____

$\frac{9}{12} - \frac{1}{3} =$ _____ $\frac{15}{16} - \frac{3}{4} =$ _____ $\frac{9}{16} - \frac{1}{2} =$ _____

Color the shapes green.

$\frac{19}{20} - \frac{1}{2} =$ _____ $\frac{7}{18} - \frac{1}{9} =$ _____ $\frac{10}{15} - \frac{2}{5} =$ _____

$\frac{5}{6} - \frac{1}{2} =$ _____ $\frac{13}{14} - \frac{2}{7} =$ _____ $\frac{5}{9} - \frac{1}{3} =$ _____

Name _____

Twirling Windmills

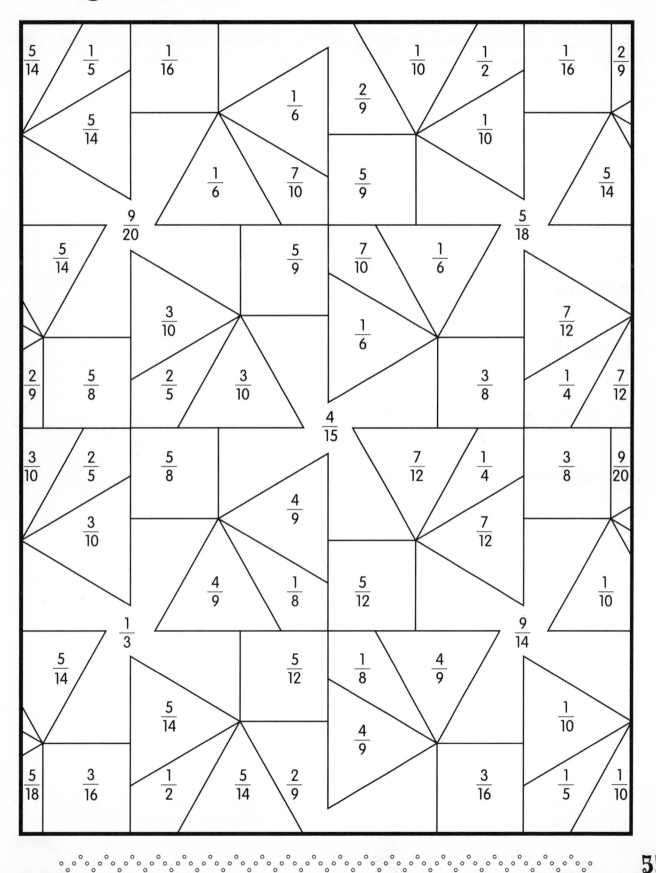

Name _____

Prairie Star

Solve the problems and rename the fractions in lowest terms. Then, on page 57, find the shape(s) with each answer, and color them as directed below. (Hint: Look carefully—some of the answers are written in more than one shape!) Finally, fill in any remaining shapes with colors of your choice.

Color the shapes dark red.

$2\frac{4}{11} + 2\frac{4}{11} =$ _____

$3\frac{1}{12} + 2\frac{6}{12} =$ _____

$1\frac{2}{7} + 4\frac{4}{7} =$ _____

Color the shapes light orange.

$2\frac{2}{4} + 2\frac{1}{4} =$ _____

$7\frac{1}{9} + 1\frac{1}{9} =$ _____

$3\frac{1}{6} + 3\frac{2}{6} =$ _____

Color the shapes blue.

$6\frac{3}{7} + 1\frac{4}{7} =$ _____

$7\frac{3}{12} + 2\frac{1}{12} =$ _____

$3\frac{2}{8} + 4\frac{1}{8} =$ _____

Color the shapes green.

$1\frac{1}{15} + 2\frac{4}{15} =$ _____

$4\frac{5}{11} + 2\frac{6}{11} =$ _____

$1\frac{2}{12} + 7\frac{3}{12} =$ _____

Color the shapes red.

$\frac{4}{10} + 1\frac{4}{10} =$ _____

$7\frac{1}{6} + 1\frac{4}{6} =$ _____

$8\frac{2}{6} + 1\frac{4}{6} =$ _____

Color the shapes yellow.

$2\frac{2}{10} + 2\frac{2}{10} =$ _____

Name _____

Prairie Star

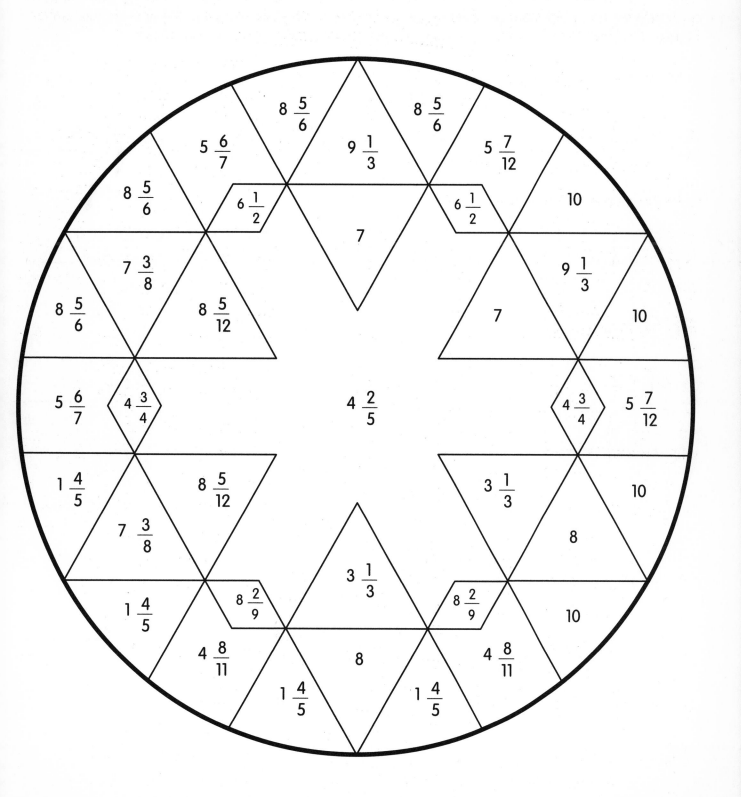

Name _____

Wagon Wheel

Solve the problems and rename the fractions in lowest terms. Then, on page 59, find the shape(s) with each answer, and color them as directed below. (Hint: Look carefully—some of the answers are written in more than one shape!) Finally, fill in any remaining shapes with colors of your choice.

Color the shapes dark red.

$4\frac{1}{2} - 2\frac{1}{2} =$ _____

$6\frac{7}{10} - 1\frac{6}{10} =$ _____

$9\frac{6}{7} - 4\frac{4}{7} =$ _____

$9\frac{4}{4} - 2\frac{1}{4} =$ _____

$7\frac{8}{9} - 5\frac{5}{9} =$ _____

$8\frac{5}{6} - 7\frac{2}{6} =$ _____

Color the shapes blue.

$9\frac{9}{12} - 1\frac{8}{12} =$ _____

$7\frac{8}{15} - 6\frac{3}{15} =$ _____

$7\frac{7}{8} - 4\frac{2}{8} =$ _____

$4\frac{4}{11} - 1\frac{1}{11} =$ _____

$7\frac{5}{13} - 2\frac{5}{13} =$ _____

$7\frac{16}{18} - 6\frac{1}{18} =$ _____

Color the shapes red.

$9\frac{5}{6} - \frac{4}{6} =$ _____

$4\frac{7}{8} - 3\frac{4}{8} =$ _____

$6\frac{5}{9} - 3\frac{4}{9} =$ _____

$8\frac{9}{14} - \frac{2}{14} =$ _____

$7\frac{9}{10} - 7\frac{2}{10} =$ _____

$9\frac{5}{6} - 1\frac{3}{6} =$ _____

Wagon Wheel

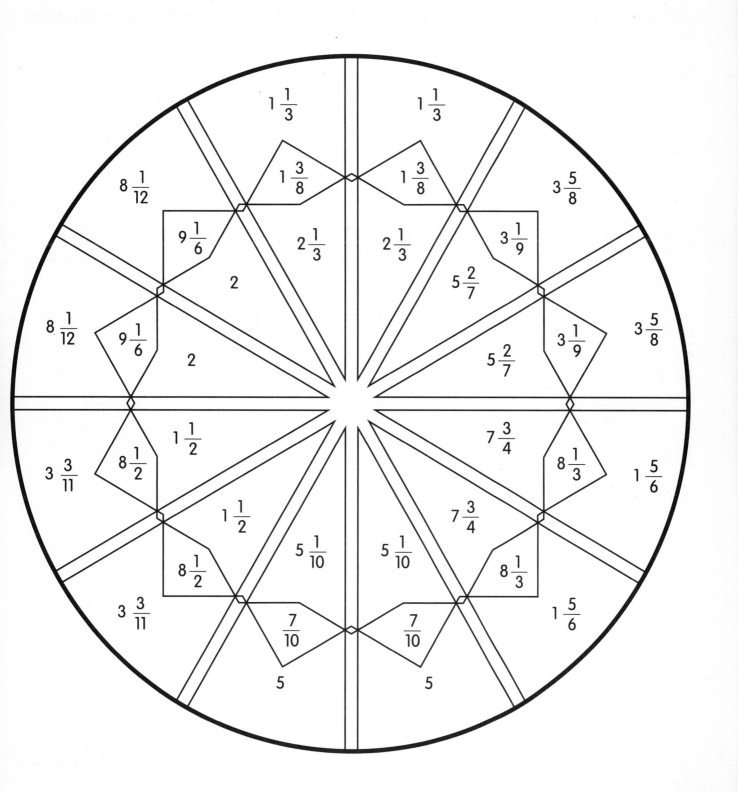

Name _____

Hexagon Puzzle

Write each decimal in fraction form. Then, on page 61, find the shape(s) with each answer, and color them as directed below. (Hint: Look carefully—some of the answers are written in more than one shape!)

Color the shapes light orange.

0.2 _____   1.2 _____   7.8 _____

Color the shapes dark red.

0.04 _____   9.22 _____   4.1 _____   7.7 _____

Color the shapes yellow.

0.92 _____   7.02 _____   7.8 _____

Color the shapes light green.

22.2 _____   6.44 _____   9.1 _____   0.4 _____

Color the shapes blue.

0.09 _____   5.25 _____   4.7 _____

Name _____

Hexagon Puzzle

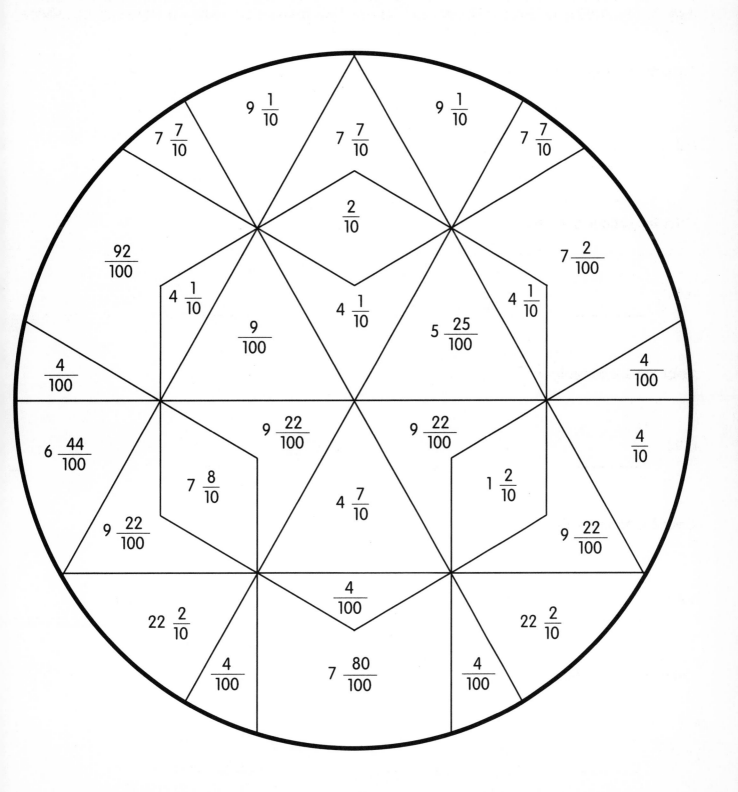

Name_____

Twinkling Lights

Write each fraction in decimal form. Then, on page 63, find the shape(s) with each answer, and color them as directed below. (Hint: Look carefully—some of the answers are written in more than one shape!) Finally, fill in any remaining shapes with colors of your choice.

Color the shapes light orange.

$\frac{2}{10}$ _____ $4\frac{2}{10}$ _____ $8\frac{7}{10}$ _____ $\frac{7}{10}$ _____

Color the shapes dark red.

$\frac{9}{100}$ _____ $\frac{74}{100}$ _____ $3\frac{3}{10}$ _____ $\frac{9}{10}$ _____

Color the shapes yellow.

$3\frac{74}{100}$ _____ $\frac{7}{100}$ _____ $3\frac{4}{10}$ _____ $\frac{1}{10}$ _____

Color the shapes light green.

$\frac{2}{100}$ _____ $5\frac{6}{100}$ _____ $9\frac{5}{10}$ _____ $\frac{34}{100}$ _____

Color the shapes blue.

$2\frac{17}{100}$ _____ $8\frac{1}{10}$ _____ $\frac{99}{100}$ _____ $9\frac{9}{100}$ _____

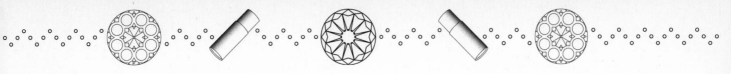

Name _____

Twinkling Lights

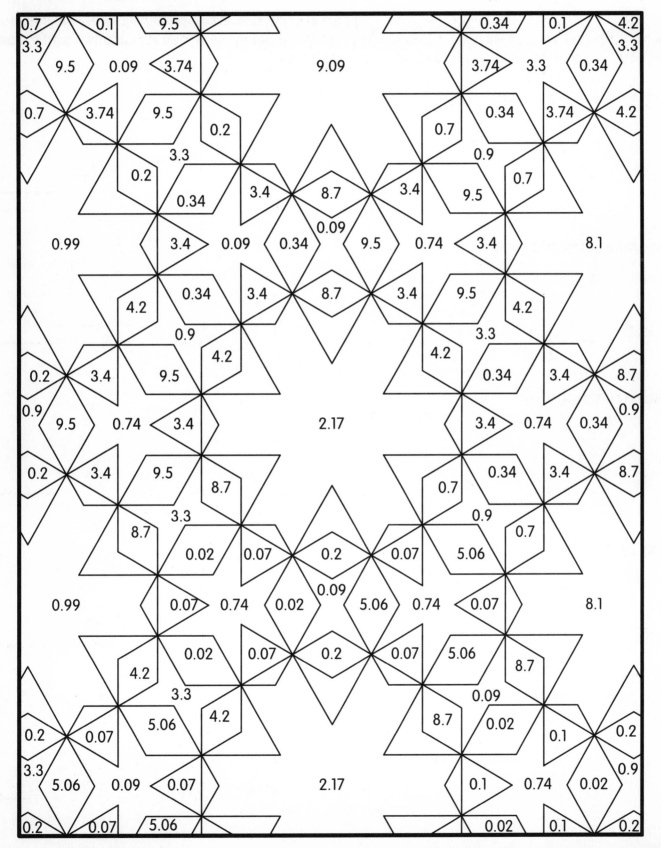

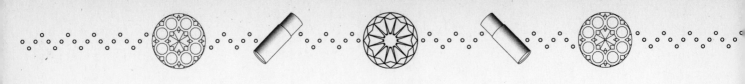